Growing Up in
Colonial America

GROWING UP IN COLONIAL AMERICA

TRACY BARRETT

THE MILLBROOK PRESS
BROOKFIELD, CONNECTICUT

Published by The Millbrook Press, Inc.
2 Old New Milford Road, Brookfield, Connecticut 06804

Cover: *Portrait of Two Children* by J. Badger, c. 1752. Photo courtesy of Abby Aldrich
Rockefeller Folk Art Center, Williamsburg, Va.

Photographs courtesy of the Library of Congress: pp. 8, 13 (bottom), 16, 18, 37, 57,
67; North Wind Picture Archives: pp. 13 (top), 28, 34, 35 (both), 39, 43, 49, 52 (both),
62, 75, 78, 81, 84; National Gallery of Art, Washington: pp. 21 (*Cradle*, by Louis
Plogsted, c. 1936), 46 (top: *Doll-"Martha"* by Rex F. Bush, c. 1937; bottom: *Rocking
Horse* by Lucille Chabot, 1935/1942); Worcester Art Museum, Worcester, Mass., Gift
of Mr. and Mrs. Albert W. Rice: p. 23; The Fine Arts Museum of San Francisco,
Gift of Mr. and Mrs. John D. Rockefeller 3rd: p. 26; The Bettmann Archive: pp. 31, 73;
The Pierpont Morgan Library, New York: p. 48 (MA 1505); Culver Pictures: pp. 60, 63.

Library of Congress Cataloging-in-Publication Data
Barrett, Tracy, 1955–
Growing up in colonial America / Tracy Barrett.
p. cm.—(American children)
Includes bibliographical references and index.
Summary: Paints a picture of life of children in the American colonies:
daily chores, routines, and play; distinct religious and social attitudes
that dictated how children were raised and what they were taught in New
England and in the South.
ISBN 1-56294-578-5
1. United States—Social life and customs—to 1775—Juvenile
literature. 2. Children—United States—History—17th century—
Juvenile literature. 3. Children—United States—History—18th
century—Juvenile literature. I. Title. II. Series.
E162B34 1995 973—dc20 94-39224 CIP AC

6

Contents

Introduction

Who was the first child of European descent to live on the North American continent? No one knows for sure. A Viking story about the discovery of Vinland (North America), written about the year 1000, says that sixty men, five women, and a herd of cattle landed in a wild country (probably Canada) and set up a small settlement there. A baby boy named Snorri was born to the leader, Karlsefni, and his wife, Gudrid. The tale says that the Vikings did not stay in Vinland very long. When their relations with the native people became difficult, they returned to their home in Greenland. If this account is true, then Snorri was the first European child in America, but his stay here was brief.

Roanoke, the mysterious "lost colony" of Virginia, was home to Virginia Dare, the first European child born in what is now the United States. She was born there in 1587, but her fate, along with that of the rest of the group, is unknown. When Virginia's grandfather returned to Roanoke after a trip back to England, everyone was gone. No one knows if Virginia lived to adulthood, perhaps joining a local native group, or if she and the rest of the colonists died that year.

When colonists boarded the *Mayflower* in 1620 and set sail from Europe for what they called the New World, 31 of the ship's 102 passengers were children. A little girl named

Pilgrims prepare to board the Mayflower at Delft Haven, Holland, in 1620. Those who remain on shore pray that the colonists will survive the fearsome crossing to the New World.

Mary Higginson died during the difficult voyage. Eight more children died during the first months in the new land, and by the end of that first harsh winter, only about half of the colonists had survived.

The first child of English ancestry born in Plymouth was named Peregrine ("Pilgrim") White. More babies were born, and new colonists continued to come to the New World. Many children survived to grow up and live out the rest of their lives in the Plymouth Colony.

Colonial children went to school, worked, played, read books, and sang songs. Many died young, since medical care was poor and life was difficult. But others lived to adulthood, and they in turn had children of their own.

Of course, children of European descent were not the only ones on the North American continent. Native Americans had lived here for thousands of years. The lives of Native American children were so different from those of the European immigrants that their story belongs in another book.

The story of African-American children is unique as well. At first, many Africans who came to the New World were indentured servants. The first boatload docked in Jamestown, Virginia, in 1619. Its passengers were bound by contract to work for a master for a set number of years. By 1641, though, the Massachusetts Colony had passed a law that allowed the enslavement of other people. From then on, most Africans who came to the colonies were brought over in chains.

Almost all the slaves at the beginning of the colonial period were adults, since children were of less use in doing the hard work slaves were forced to do. And the captives were so weakened by the terrible conditions they suffered on the voyage from Africa that they often had a hard time having children. But in 1624, the first African American, William Tucker, was born in Jamestown. By 1649, there were about three hundred African and African-American slaves in Virginia alone.

Less is known about the lives of African-American children in the colonies than about European-American children. Almost all of the writers of the colonial period were white, and most of them did not believe that the lives of blacks, either slave or free, were worth mentioning. And African Americans left fewer physical traces of their lives. Slaves and free blacks usually had to make do with the worn-out shoes, clothes, toys, and tools of white people. These items were in such poor shape that they were used until they were thrown away. So, many details about the daily lives of this part of the population have been lost.

If you were to speak with one of the colonists, would you understand each other? Probably. Most of them came from England, and although our language has changed some since then, the two of you would still be able to hold a conversation. It did not take long for people from other countries to start flooding in, however. By the time of the Revolution, about half the people who had immigrated to the colonies were of non-English background (including about one fifth of the population that was of African origin). With people coming from so many different places, different cultures existed side by side and gradually began to influence one another. English is full of words borrowed from other languages, as a result of the colonists' struggle to communicate with each other.

Who were the children of the American colonies? How did they spend their days? Would a child from modern America recognize their games, their schoolbooks, their homes? Would you be comfortable with the food, the living conditions, the family relations of the young people who lived here before you? These questions and more will be explored here.

PART ONE

LIFE IN THE COLONIES

The people who came to the American colonies from Europe were from many countries and cultural traditions. They also had different reasons for leaving Europe:

Some had a religious or political purpose for coming to the New World. People were often forbidden to practice their religion in their home countries. They were seeking a new land where they would be free to follow whatever beliefs they chose. This is why the Quakers and Puritans came, as well as the Separatists, or Pilgrims, the group of Puritans who settled in Plymouth.

Others were concerned that Native Americans were not Christians. Convinced that they must save the souls of the "heathens," missionaries braved the difficult trip across the ocean to convert them to Christianity. Still other immigrants had grown tired of the power of the kings or princes in their homelands. They hoped to create a new form of government in the new land, one that would be fair to all.

Many Europeans immigrated for more practical reasons. Some wished to own land. In most of Europe, the amount of land that could be farmed was limited. In the seventeenth century, the world was just starting to come out of the "little Ice Age," and the temperature was much lower than it is now. In many areas, it was too cold to grow crops. To prevent the farms that did exist from being broken up, the law said that only the oldest son of the family could inherit his father's land. Any remaining sons had to choose another profession (daughters were expected to marry and be supported by their husbands). Some of these young men wanted to farm instead of finding something else to do, and so they came to try their luck in the wide-open spaces of America. Many of them were excited by the adventure of living in what they saw as an untamed land.

Some people had no real choice in crossing the ocean. Among these were criminals from Europe who had been forced to choose between going to jail or going to America. Others were slaves who were captured and taken to the Americas, where they labored at building settlements and clearing land to farm. Most of these slaves were Africans, although there were also indentured servants from Europe at the time.

Most of the children who came to America were members of a family, but even as early as the *Mayflower*, a few orphans were among the passengers. There was also at least one runaway on the *Mayflower*: a sixteen-year-old boy who decided to leave home when his father whipped him for taking dancing lessons. Some parents sent their mischievous children to America in the hope that the rough life there would calm them down and teach them some responsibility.

Of course, with such a mix of people with so many reasons for starting over in a new land, life in any one European settlement in America differed from life in any other. Also, the climate and soil influenced how people lived. The first settlements were on the east coast, and ranged from chilly New England to hot and

A Quaker meeting in England. The Quakers came to the colonies to escape persecution for practicing their religion.

Africans are brought ashore from a Dutch man-of-war at Jamestown in 1619. Slavery would soon take hold in the colonies and continue, particularly in the South, for more than two hundred years.

humid Florida. The land in the central part, in what is now Virginia, Maryland, and the Carolinas, was fertile and fairly easy to cultivate. In the north, though, the rocky soil was a challenge to even the most experienced farmer.

At first, the two major areas of settlement by the mostly English settlers were along the coast, one in Plymouth, Massachusetts, and the other along the Chesapeake Bay of Maryland and Virginia. If you were to visit these early settlements, what would you find? Let's go back now three hundred years and see.

The
First Homes

๛

The colonists first settled on land that had already been cleared by the Native Americans who farmed near the coast. Shelters were built as quickly as possible to protect the colonists from the cold and the unfamiliar animals. In some cases, the new arrivals merely moved their few possessions into caves that Indians had used and abandoned. Or they used sailcloth to make tents. Some managed to lash together logs and branches to make crude huts. As time went on, people built more permanent homes out of wood and stone, both of which were easy to find in the new land.

In Plymouth, people tried to make their houses and towns as similar as possible to what they had left behind in England. Unfortunately, many of them had come from big cities and had no idea how to build a house or to farm or hunt. But they did the best they could, and as one learned a skill, it would be passed on to a neighbor. They patterned the plan of their villages on an English country town. The houses lined up neatly along a central street, and their fields were a short walking distance beyond. The street widened at the end to a "green," or "common," where animals could graze. Of course, the church was built early in the settlement, since the Pilgrims felt that religion was the most im-

Leyden Street, in Plymouth. The first New England villages were fashioned after the English villages that the colonists had left behind.

portant part of their lives. It was not until the eighteenth century that some towns became large enough to be called cities.

Since they had to get established quickly and protect themselves from bad weather, the first Pilgrims could not take the time to make their houses large and comfortable. They lived in small, unpainted huts about twenty feet by twenty feet. There was no real floor, just hard-packed dirt. The houses had to be in the full sunshine to keep the roof shingles dry so they would not rot, and the houses were very hot in the summer. There usually was only one story, but a larger house might have a sleeping loft that was reached by a ladder.

There were no real windows. Shutters, used today mostly for decoration, were important to keep out the cold wind in the winter. The doorways were small, also to keep out the wind, and sometimes even children had to stoop when they entered. Indoors, there was little furniture and only rarely was there any decoration.

Every house had a kitchen garden and orchard to supply the most necessary foods. What one person did not grow, someone else probably did, and most people traded produce with each other. Since the houses were so small, each room had to serve several purposes. The main room served as the kitchen, the dining room, the living room, and the work- shop. People would sleep wherever their bedrolls would fit. Later, beds were made of different heights, and the lower bed (the trundle) could be pushed under the higher one to save space during the day. And of course there were no bathrooms. Everyone, rich or poor, young or old, free or slave, had to use an outhouse.

In the Chesapeake area, the settlers were not as con- cerned with re-creating their old lives. They built their houses in the middle of their large tobacco fields, to make it easier to tend the crops. They also built some churches, but

Families lived in roughly built one-room huts. Here, a man shares kernels of corn, a woman cooks, and a baby sleeps in a cradle. The ladder leads to a sleeping loft, a luxury that many of the earliest houses did not have.

not as quickly as the Plymouth settlers. Most of the Chesapeake settlers practiced Christianity—they were Anglicans, members of the established Church of England. But they had come to the New World to make money quickly, not necessarily to build churches—or even to establish a new colony.

The houses they built were dark inside. Many of them had only one room, with a large fireplace at one end. It was more important to keep the cold out than to let the light in, so the windows (if there were any) were just narrow slits cut into the walls. These holes might be covered with oiled paper or very thin slices of an animal's horn, which would let some dim light in. As a rule, colonial people did not care to have homes with a view. The outdoors was frightening, full of strange beasts and people with whom they could not speak very well. It was also where they spent most of their days in backbreaking work. When they were in their houses, they wanted to feel safe and removed from the outside world.

What light there was usually came from the fire. If someone had work to do that needed extra light—making a piece of furniture, knitting a pair of mittens, tending a sick baby—some dry wood would be thrown on the fire to brighten the room for a short while. Candles were expensive to buy and difficult to make, so it was a long time before people used them regularly. Sometimes people burned whale-oil lamps, but the oil had to be brought from England or bought from whalers, so once again, most people learned to do without. When it got dark, people went to bed because they had to get up very early the next day.

Bringing
Up Babies

❦

The people of the colonies brought with them from Europe their ideas of how children should be raised. They believed that babies were just lumps of flesh whose parents had to shape them into human beings, both their bodies and their souls. First, the midwife who helped the mother give birth would lay the newborn baby flat on her lap and press her hands all over its face, smoothing it out, pulling the tiny nose to make it longer, like the nose of an adult, and squeezing together the bones of the head to try to make the soft spot on top close up sooner. Then the baby's arms and legs would be straightened out and firmly wrapped.

People believed that if babies were allowed to develop naturally, they would never learn to walk upright. Thus from a very early age, babies wore a corset, a kind of undershirt stiffened with whalebone or other hard material, and a stiff board was strapped onto their back to keep it absolutely straight. Crawling was forbidden, because only animals went around on all fours, while people walked upright. So both boys and girls were dressed in long robes and several layers of petticoats. These were worn partly to keep the babies warm in winter, but also to make it harder for them to crawl. They also used a device similar to a modern baby walker, but with no seat. Babies were strapped into it and forced to stay on their feet. If they grew tired and screamed, they were ignored; adults thought that babies couldn't really feel pain or discomfort and that, in any case, they cried in order to exercise their lungs. They also thought that the first lesson children should learn was to be obedient in all things, and if an adult wanted them to stand, they had to stand, no matter what.

When it was possible, babies spent the first few weeks of their lives with their mothers. Childbirth was a dangerous time for both mother and baby, so the other members of the

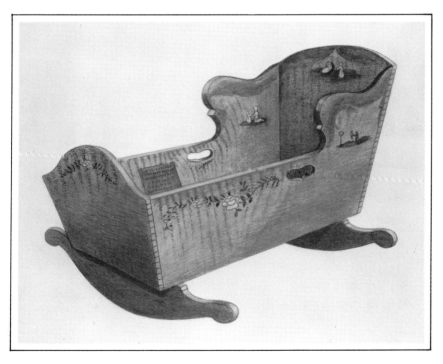

A cradle from Kentucky, built about 1704.

family ran the household, allowing the two of them to rest and recover. Of course, some families could not afford to let an adult member take a few weeks off. Farm women, for example, had to get on their feet again as soon as possible to get back to their important work. And slave mothers were forced to return to work very soon. It was considered generous to allow them to shorten their workday a little in order to take care of their new baby.

It was especially important to the Puritans of New England to make sure that the child lived long enough to be baptized. Their religion taught them that a child dying before baptism would go straight to Hell.

When babies started to walk, busy parents could not keep a careful watch over them to protect them from falls. So they were often fitted with a cap that was thickly padded to protect them from falls. This big round hat was called a "pudding." (Today, people still affectionately call a little child "puddin' head"!) Both boys and girls wore a long robe that opened in the front, with ribbons hanging from the shoulders for decoration. They wore a hat in most weather (even the summer was cooler than it is now, especially in the North), and in the winter they would wear two or three at a time.

Some babies probably slept in cradles; but with so much work to do, it was more common for busy parents to use whatever materials were at hand to make a sleeping place: a box, a crate, a few boards hastily nailed together. The baby had to be kept warm, so during the day this makeshift cradle was left near the fireplace (with straps covering the top so the baby wouldn't roll out), and at night the baby

"Mrs. Freake and Baby Mary," by an unknown Massachusetts artist, 1674.

would sleep with the parents, either in their bed or in a cradle next to it. There were very few high chairs or other special furniture for children. There simply was no time or energy to make special furniture that would be used for such a short while.

When they were very small, babies were usually bathed once a day, but as they grew older, they were washed once a week or so, like the rest of the family. Their diapers were not changed often, since washing water was scarce. This meant that they suffered badly from diaper rash, and parents traded recipes for creams and ointments to soothe their babies' irritated skin.

Babyhood was short in the colonies. By the age of three, most children were expected to help out the family: They might weed the garden, feed the chickens, or wash the dishes. At four, both boys and girls were taught to knit. Children were given chores not only to make them feel useful, but because their help was really needed.

How Clothes
Were Made

ℰ◊ℬ

By the time they turned five or six—the age when children today are just entering kindergarten—colonial children reached a new stage in their lives, too. At this age, boys were treated differently from girls for the first time. Boys were "breeched," that is, put into their first pair of pants. This was often a real occasion, with friends and relatives invited to see the "little man" in his first adult clothes. Both boys and girls were given shoes to wear. They had always worn slippers in cold weather, but now they were expected to do real work both indoors and out and their feet needed more protection. Usually these shoes were of soft leather, like moccasins, but children from more wealthy families wore store-bought shoes with hard soles, at first imported from Europe. They were usually fastened shut with buttons. Boys might also have a pair of boots.

For almost everyone, store-bought clothes made of fine materials were too expensive. Instead, most people made their own clothes. Fortunately, they could find materials for clothing almost everywhere around them. Cotton grew well in the South, and flax for making linen was soon planted in most of the colonies. Sheep brought over from Europe— although they needed constant watching because of the dan-

"The Mason Children: David, Joanna, and Abigail," by an unknown artist in Massachusetts, 1670. All of their clothes—even the material, thread, hooks, and buttons—were made by hand.

ger from wolves, bears, and mountain lions—became plentiful, and their wool was used to make warm winter clothes. Buttons were sometimes carved from wood, and they were also made from hardened leather, cow or sheep horns, and deer antlers.

It took a lot of work to make clothes, and children were involved in almost every step along the way. Imagine how much time it took to make one simple linen shirt: To begin, the flax (a long, thin plant that grew well in wet areas) had to be planted, at first with precious seeds brought over from Europe, and later with seeds from these original plants. The young shoots were so tender that the people weeding them had to walk barefoot so they wouldn't trample them, and they had to work facing the wind, so any plants they accidentally bent down in front of them as they went would be blown upright. Children often did this work, since they were shorter than adults and so didn't have to bend as far to reach the plants. Also, their small feet were less likely to damage the fragile flax. After the plants had reached their full height, they were harvested, with great care taken to preserve the seeds for planting the next year, and to make the prized flaxseed oil. Next, the stalks were beaten to remove the soft part of the plant, leaving the long, tough fibers (something like the "threads" in a stalk of celery) behind. These were chopped and left to dry. The fibers, called "tow" (pronounced "toh"), were soft and pale yellow (we still call someone with very pale-blond hair a "towhead"). The tow was then gathered up and spun into long threads.

One of little girls' (and some little boys') first "grown-up" jobs was spinning. Every house had a spinning wheel, and very few days would go by without its humming filling the house. The flax fibers were strong and could hurt the hands unless the spinner took great care with the spinning wheel. This was a long job, and one that every child had to learn how to do. In 1640, in fact, the court of the Massachusetts

A girl works at her spinning wheel while food warms in a pot hanging over the fire. Spinning was a daily chore for most colonial girls.

Colony passed a law saying that *every* child in the colony had to learn to spin both flax and wool.

Once the thread had been spun, it had to be bleached. It was soaked in various liquids until it was white enough for its purpose: cream colored for a work shirt, bright white for a baby's christening robe. Sometimes the cloth was dyed. The colonists had brought some dyes with them, and quickly learned from the Indians and by experimentation which local plants could be used to make dyes of different colors.

Children from wealthy families had a lot of clothes, and some special ones for dressing up. Near the end of the seventeenth century, a ten-year-old boy going to boarding school in New England brought with him:

Eleven new shirts
4 pair laced sleves
8 Plane Cravats
4 Cravats with Lace
4 Stripte Wastecoats with black buttons
1 Flowered Wastecoat
4 New osenbrig [linen] britches
1 Gray hat with a black ribbon
1 Gray hat with a blew ribbon
1 Dousin black buttons
1 Dousin coloured buttons
3 Pair gold buttons
3 Pair silver buttons
2 Pair Fine blew Stockings
1 Pair Fine red Stockings
4 white Handkerchiefs
2 speckled Handkerchiefs
5 Pair Gloves
1 Stuff Coat with black buttons
1 Cloth Coat
1 Pair blew plush britches
1 Pair Serge britches
2 Combs
1 pair new Shooes
Silk and Thred

List quoted from Alice Morse Earle's *Home Life in Colonial Days* (1898)

The parents of a young girl in Virginia in 1737 could not find clothes elegant enough for their daughter locally, so they ordered the following items from England:

A cap ruffle and tucker, the lace 5 shillings per Yard
1 pair White Stays
8 pair White Kid gloves
2 pair coloured kid gloves
2 pair worsted hose
3 pair thread hose
1 pair silk shoes laced
1 pair morocco shoes
1 Hoop Coat
1 Hat
4 pair plain Spanish shoes
2 pair calf shoes
1 mask
1 fan
1 necklace
1 Girdle and buckle
1 piece fashionable Calico
4 yards ribbon for knots
½ yard Cambric
A mantua [cloak] and coat of lute-string

List quoted from Alice Morse Earle's *Child Life in Colonial Days* (1932)

The native dyes came from nutshells, barks, and berries and made mostly shades of yellow and brown. Indigo, a blue imported from the West Indies, and madder root, which made a bright red and was also imported, were saved for special occasions. The dye was boiled for hours and then strained, after which the thread was placed in it and stirred. It was then removed, dried, and woven into cloth.

Many houses had looms, and children too young to work them alone helped in the weaving by stringing the threads, passing the heavy shuttle back and forth, and snipping off loose ends with scissors. Once the cloth was woven, it was cut out and sewn into clothes. Buttonholes were carefully worked in, and the buttons were sewn on.

Most of the work of sewing was done by girls and women. It was very important for girls to practice making different kinds of stitches and be able to do them well before they were trusted with the work of making a whole article of clothing. To help them practice, their mothers often assigned them a task, such as sewing a seam six inches long before suppertime or working eight neat buttonholes after church. When they had learned all the stitches, many girls were given the task of covering a piece of cloth with a design made of the different stitches. Since this cloth showed a sample of many stitches, it was called a "sampler." Girls worked for weeks and even months on a sampler, and it was a special day in her life when she successfully completed it— the day she had proven she could be trusted to sew clothing for herself and her family.

Cloth made with so much effort, or later bought with so much expense, could obviously not be wasted. Worn-out

A sampler from 1773. Its religious and educational motifs were typical of samplers made in colonial times.

clothes were carefully preserved, and when enough scraps had been saved, the girls and women cut them up and made them into patchwork quilts. If they were in a hurry, they just sewed them together in any way that they would fit, but many beautiful patterns were invented by creative women and girls in the colonies.

When all the pieces had been joined together, the women and children in the neighborhood were invited over for a "quilting bee." The pieced layer, a stuffing made of cotton or other soft material, and a bottom layer would be stitched together to form a quilt. The women and older girls sat around the edges of the quilt, sewing and talking. For many of them, this was the only time aside from church that a large group could get together. News was passed on, and gossip was repeated. Anyone invited to a quilting bee would be sure to go, or she would probably wind up being talked about by her neighbors! The children had important duties to perform. They had to keep a good supply of needles threaded, and pass them on to the quilters as they used up their thread. The smaller children sat underneath the quilt, and as the needle came down, they pulled it through and then pushed it back up to the seamstress.

Household Chores

Children did much more than just sewing, however. Abigail Foote, a young girl in Connecticut, wrote a diary in 1775 where she listed some of her activities:

> Fix'd gown for Prude,—Mend Mother's Riding-hood,—Spun short thread,—Fix'd two gowns for Welsh's girls,—Carded [Smoothed] tow,—Spun linen,—Worked on Cheese-basket,—Hatchel'd [Chopped] flax with Hannah, we did 51 lbs. apiece,—Pleated and ironed,—Read a Sermon of Dodridge's—Spooled a piece,—Milked the cows,—Spun linen, did 50 knots,—Made a Broom of Guinea wheat straw,—Spun thread to whiten,—Set a Red dye,—Had two Scholars from Mrs. Taylor's,—I carded two pounds of whole wool and felt Nationly,—Spun harness twine,—Scoured the pewter.

Not only clothes, but almost everything the families used each day was made at home. As soon as they were able, children helped with every chore. Making soap, for example, was a long process. It started with someone's collecting wood ashes from the fireplace and putting them in a barrel with small holes punched in the bottom. Water was then poured slowly over the ashes, and the water dripped through and was collected in a basin underneath. This ash water, called lye, had to be thick enough to float an egg; if the egg

Making soap from lye was a messy process best done outdoors.

sank, the process had to be repeated. The lye was then mixed with animal fat, and the resulting soft jelly was soap. Surprisingly, it was neither dirty like ashes nor greasy like animal fat, and did a very good job of cleaning clothes and skin.

In exploring the new plants around them, the settlers soon found a bush they called the "bayberry," whose berries could be boiled and produce a kind of wax that made a very sweet-smelling candle. Children's small fingers were very useful when it came to collecting the tiny berries. But this was a long process, and candles produced with bayberries were saved for special occasions. The lucky person who managed to track a bee down to its tree found not only honey but also beeswax that could be used for making fine candles as well as for polishing furniture.

If bayberry or beeswax was unavailable, animal fat could also be used in making candles. Scraps of fat were saved and melted slowly together to make tallow. Even young children could learn how to twist pieces of cotton thread together to make wicks and then string them over long sticks. All the carefully saved tallow was then melted and kept warm. The strings were dipped into the tallow pot, and then quickly removed and allowed to cool. When they had hardened, the wicks were once again dipped in the tallow to make a second layer. Timing was important—if the wicks were left in too long, all the tallow that had been built up earlier would melt off. The dipping was repeated until the candles were as thick as the candle dipper wanted.

It was not many years before candlemakers began to travel through the colonies, stopping at people's houses with their large candle molds. These molds would be set up in the kitchen, and wicks placed inside them. Then the wax or tallow saved by the family would be slowly poured into the molds, and when it was cooled the mold would be opened and the candles removed.

Children often helped in the painstaking chore of making candles from tallow, scraps of melted fat. When molds for making candles came into use (right), at least one household task took less time.

What People Ate

The colonists were famous for loving sweets: European visitors often commented on how bad their teeth were. Getting sugar from plants was a long, hot process, and most sugar had to be imported in the form of a hard loaf from Europe. The Native Americans taught the colonists how to make syrup from the sap of the maple tree, but the sugar maple did not grow all over the colonies, and boiling the sap to make the syrup was as long and hot as making sugar. Honey, on the other hand, is ready to eat as soon as it is found. Sometimes someone would be lucky enough to spot bees flying in and out of a bee tree, but usually a child would be sent to find one when the family ran low on honey. He would set a dish of sweetened water out in a field and wait until a bee found it. When the bee had drunk its fill and had started back to the hive, the child would follow it until he lost sight of the bee. Then he would set the dish down until another bee came and would follow that one. Eventually a bee would lead him to the tree, and then the child's job was over. The adults would have the difficult and dangerous job of smoking the bees out of their hive.

Everything the colonists ate had to come from the land. Boys, and sometimes girls, were given guns at a very young

A late colonial farmyard scene. Even young children joined in hunting, fishing, gathering, and cultivating food for the family table.

age (six or seven was not unusual) and taught to shoot. When young, they could go hunting for small animals near their homes. Possums, squirrels, raccoons, rabbits—a child could shoot one of these and carry it home without help. When they got a little older, boys could join the men on a longer hunt, looking for deer or even bears. Just as with the women and their quilting bees, the men used hunting expeditions as an opportunity to get together and become reacquainted with each other. At the same time, the boys learned from them the tasks they would need to be responsible for as they got older.

Most early settlements were along the ocean, and even as people went inland, they needed to settle near water. Children went fishing and dug in the sand for clams and oysters.

Aside from providing much-needed food for the family table, days spent fishing were often a special treat, and children would swim and picnic when they had caught enough fish.

The colonists brought over seeds of crops that they wished to plant in their new home. Among the first European crops to be successfully grown were apples and peaches. Both boys and girls had to help with planting, weeding, and harvesting these precious crops. They looked forward to apple-picking time, when they were finally allowed to climb the trees and pick the ripe fruit, eating as much as they wanted in the process. There were also many fruits and vegetables in the New World that were strange to the colonists. No one in Europe had ever seen squash or pumpkins before, but the colonists were told by the Native Americans that they were good to eat, and they soon became an important part of the diet. One colonist even complained,

> We have pumpkins at morning and pumpkins at noon,
> If it were not for pumpkins we should be undone.

Tomatoes and potatoes were also new, and at first the Europeans could not be persuaded to eat them, since they thought they were poisonous. In fact, they were partly right: The stems and leaves of these plants can indeed make you very sick. After a time they learned what parts were edible, and when they had gotten used to them, they did eat them. In the South, sweet potatoes were accepted quickly. But although these plants were easily grown in their native soil, they were not highly regarded at first and were usually eaten only when no meat could be had. In England, people who ate vegetables were looked down upon, since it was

Corn was husked and pumpkins gathered in the fall. Native Americans introduced the colonists to these foods, which soon became part of almost every meal.

thought that only the poor who couldn't afford meat ate vegetables. This custom was carried into the New World. But the more adventurous experimented with local foods.

The first American cookbook was *The Compleat House-wife*, written by William Parks and published in Virginia in 1742. He said that he would not include recipes "the Ingredients or Materials for which, are not to be had in this Country," by which he meant the Chesapeake area. A different attitude was taken by Susannah Carter, whose 1772 *The Frugal Housewife* (with illustrations by Paul Revere) did not include anything made with American beans, corn, squash, cranberries, or pumpkin. She did, however, mention turkey, potatoes, and turtle, all of which were important parts of the American diet. By 1796, new kinds of food from America were so established that in Amelia Simmons's *American Cookery* there are recipes for cookies (from the Dutch word *koekje*, or "small cake") and slaw (also from Dutch: *sla*, or "salad"), both of which were new words in English. She gives many recipes using potatoes, saying that these vegetables "take rank for universal use, profit, and easy acquirement." She even gives a recipe for a potato-pudding dessert!

Very few homes had a separate kitchen or dining room, or even a dinner table. Some boards were laid across a packing case brought over from Europe, or on top of a workbench, and benches and stools were pulled up next to them. This was the table. When the meal was over, it was taken apart again. Most food was served in bowls and eaten with spoons. Knives had sharp points; after the meat was sliced with them, the food was speared with the point of the knife and eaten off it. When forks first came from Europe in the eighteenth century, most people thought they were an unnecessary luxury.

Preparing food took a lot of time. Everything had to be made by hand. Making butter, for example, would take all day. Milk would be heated and then poured into shallow pans to cool. The cream would slowly rise to the top and be skimmed off. Someone would pour the cream into a tall butter churn with a handle coming out of a hole in the top. Then they would take turns pumping this handle up and down until the small lumps of butter started to form. This

Many of the recipes in colonial cookbooks sound like they would taste good to us today. From Susannah Carter's 1772 *The Frugal Housewife:*

GOOD FRITTERS

Mix half a pint of good cream, very thick with flour, beat six eggs, leaving out four whites, and to the eggs put six spoonfuls of sack [sherry wine], and strain them into the batter; put in a little grated nutmeg, ginger and cinnamon, all very fine, also a little salt, then put in another half pint of cream, and beat the batter near an hour; pare and slice your apples very thin, dip every piece in the batter, and throw them into a pan full of boiling lard.

Colonial people enjoyed eating and sharing their hospitality with their friends. A visitor to the Virginia area was obviously overwhelmed by how much food he was offered:

> Their Breakfast Tables have generally the cold Remains of the former Day, hash'd or fricasseed; Coffee, Tea, Chocolate, Venison-pastry, Punch, and Beer, or Cyder, upon one Board; their Dinner, good Beef, Veal, Mutton, Venison, Turkies and Geese, wild and tame, Fowls, boil'd and roasted, and perhaps somewhat more, as Pies, Puddings, &c., for dessert: Suppers the same, with some small Addition, and a good hearty Cup to precede a Bed of Down: And this is the constant life they lead, and to this Fare every Comer is welcome.

was a long process, and every child tall enough to reach the churn would have to take part. Then the milk would be carefully poured through a strainer. The butter lumps stayed in the strainer, and the buttermilk that poured through the strainer was saved. If there was too much for the family to drink or use in cooking, it would be fed to the hogs. The yellow butter would be shaped into balls with long wooden paddles. It took a lot of practice to make a nice ball instead of a formless blob. The butter and cheese, which was also made at home, had to be used right away or kept in a cool place, sometimes a small house built over a stream.

Food was cooked on the fireplace in the main room. Wood was easy to find. Young children quickly learned how to start a fire and how to keep it burning. If the fire accidently went out, a child would be sent to a neighbor's house with a shovel to "beg a fire": to ask for a hot coal from the neighbor's fire. The coal would be placed on the shovel and covered with small pieces of wood or straw and the child would walk quickly back home, taking care not to spill the precious coal. If the coal was still glowing when the child got home, it would be placed in the fireplace and carefully fed small pieces of wood until it began to burn again. If no neighbor lived near enough to supply a coal, a lump of stone called a "flint" and a piece of steel would be struck together until a spark flew out onto a piece of straw. The person making the fire would have to blow on it very gently to keep the spark alive and then slowly feed it larger and larger pieces of wood. This was a long, tedious job, sometimes requiring hours. So the child whose job was to tend the fire took this responsibility very seriously.

At first, pots and pans were brought over from England. They were made of heavy metal, usually iron. Most pans had long handles to protect the cook's hands from the heat and her face from the sparks. The fireplace had no oven for baking, so the dough for a pie or loaf of bread would be placed on the edge of the hearth and covered with a metal pan to make a miniature oven. Of course, it was difficult to be sure of the exact temperature of the fire, so the food had to be checked frequently. Children could do this job, as well

A girl gathers apples from the family orchard.

as turning meat on a spit and making the cornmeal mush that everyone seemed to eat at least once a day.

Breakfast was usually a bowl of cornmeal mush, sometimes served with milk and perhaps sweetened with maple syrup or honey. Dinner, in the middle of the day, was a stew of whatever meat and vegetables were on hand. Supper was another bowl of mush. People were afraid to drink water, because even though they did not know about germs, they recognized that sometimes people got sick after drinking dirty water. In the early colonial period they did not yet know about coffee, tea, or chocolate (the first chocolate factory in America opened in 1705), and milk was scarce at first, since cows did not do well in the relatively uncleared land. Fruit juice, especially cider, and beer and rum were common drinks.

There were lots of fruits from which to make juice. Almost every family had an orchard where they grew apples and cherries. Although there were some grapes already growing in the Americas, the colonists brought over seeds of the kinds of grapes they already knew and liked. Berries grew wild all over, and cranberries and blueberries, new to the colonists, quickly became popular both for eating and for juice. Children looked forward to berry-picking time, since they were allowed to eat as many berries as they wanted while picking them.

Although food was abundant during the warm months, winter was another matter. Animals grew scarce as their food supplies were covered with snow, and some fish retreated to the deeper, warmer waters. In the deepest cold, meat could be hung from a tree, out of reach of hungry dogs, bears, wolves, and other animals. Smoking fish and meat over a wood fire would preserve it. Another way to keep meat for a long time was to pack it in salt, although salt was expensive and hard to find. No wonder that so much space in the early cookbooks was devoted to the processes of pickling and preserving!

Free Time

Life was certainly difficult, and it is not surprising that people needed to relax and play games from time to time. Even the Puritans and Quakers, who were so concerned with raising their children strictly, made or bought toys for them. They convinced themselves, however, that their children "are often thinking of Christ, while they are at their play." Other colonists were less concerned with the religious side of playing.

At first, children had few real toys to play with. Their parents were so busy trying to stay alive that they did not have the time to make something as impractical as a doll or a toy gun. Still, children managed to find toys all around them. Barrels that brought supplies from Europe were used until they were falling apart, and then the children were allowed to take the hoops that held the long straight sides together and play with them. A child who could roll a hoop all the way home from school was a real champion. Small stones were good for marbles, or for jacks, if anyone was lucky enough to have a rubber ball. Cat's cradle required only a length of string, and hopscotch was easy to play with pebbles on a smooth surface. Some children kept pets: cats, dogs, and birds. Parents who could afford them bought dolls, tea sets, and dollhouses that were at first imported from Europe, and later made in the colonies. The earliest surviving

This 1730 doll is made from papier-mâché and wood. Children often made their own out of straw and cloth.

A colonial family brought this rocking horse with them from England.

colonial dollhouse dates from 1744, but others were certainly made before this one.

Books were very expensive and were treasured by the few people lucky enough to own more than a Bible. The first book published in America, in 1646, was written for children, and was called *Milk for Babes*. Like most other books for children of that time, it was not for amusement but for education. It gave religious lessons and told children how to behave. Another example of the kind of book children would read is the 1714 *A Devout Contemplation on the Meaning of Divine Providence in the Early Death of Pious and Lovely Children*. Not only children, but also adults, were supposed to be inspired by reading about the holy lives led by these little children, all of whom died young! Other books were probably more entertaining. Both adults and children loved *Aesop's Fables*, *Pilgrim's Progress*, *Robinson Crusoe*, *Gulliver's Travels*, and *Mother Goose*. Many of these books had to be brought over from England. In the evenings, people would gather in the main room and sew, knit, spin, or whittle while someone read to them from one of these books. It was an important day when mail arrived from Europe, bringing not only letters with news of friends and relatives but also, for the lucky ones, new books to read.

There was, of course, no television, not even radio. The Puritans did not approve of music outside the church, but other groups enjoyed listening to fiddles and to keyboard instruments such as the virginal, the spinet, and the harpsichord (the piano was not yet invented). Most churches had hymns to sing during the services, and even the stricter religions allowed people to sing or hum these tunes as they went

Children listen to Contes de Ma Mere Loye, French for "Mother Goose Stories." Storytelling was common, since books were scarce.

about their daily business. Troupes of actors roamed the area by the end of the seventeenth century, and it was a real treat to be taken to see a play, although Puritans frowned on this amusement as being ungodly.

Many of the sports popular with the colonial Americans seem cruel to us today. When a convicted criminal was punished in public, children would be given a holiday from school, and adults would stop working to go and watch the whipping, dunking in a cold pond, or even execution. They

Boys appear amused at the sight of a man who has been put in the stocks for some misdeed. Puritans believed in making people suffer in public for their crimes.

were supposed to learn the lesson that "crime does not pay" from watching the punishments, but there is no doubt that most people found the sight very entertaining. It was also thought fun to make two animals fight each other and gamble on which one would win. Two dogs, two roosters, or a dog and a bull would be turned out into a ring and everyone would cheer wildly while they attacked each other, sometimes fighting to the death. The owner of a champion dog or rooster could make a lot of money off the bets. Not only adults, but children too, would go to these contests.

In fact, there were not many differences between how children and adults behaved. They all worked hard and had little time for fun. Much of childhood was spent in learning the skills necessary for adult life. When young people married and set up their own homes, they already knew how to do most of the work that was required. Almost all of them had grown up on farms and had been learning the skills necessary to survive in the New World from the time they could walk. By 1776, there were 2.5 million colonists in the thirteen states. Only 100,000 of them lived in cities. These city people were often recent immigrants from Europe who brought over the skills in manufacturing, printing, and other industries that the new country was going to need as it set off on its own.

PART TWO

DIFFERENT WAYS OF LIFE

When we think of the early colonists in America, it is usually the pilgrims in the Plymouth Bay Colony that come to mind. Much of our American way of life—our democratic government, our system of education, and many of our social attitudes—can be traced back to them.

However, these immigrants were not the only colonists by any means. Enslaved Africans, convicts who had to choose between prison and the colonies, indentured servants, farmers, and tradespeople from many countries in Europe—all of these people together created our colonial heritage.

The following chapters will focus on the beliefs and attitudes that shaped family relationships, social life, and education within the two largest colonial settlements. After visiting Plymouth and seeing how children were raised according to its strict religious principles, we will travel to Chesapeake to learn about the harsh realities that faced the earliest settlers and how southern attitudes about raising children differed from those in the North.

Most black people came to the colonies in chains, and many of them did the backbreaking work of clearing the land and harvesting the first crops on tobacco farms in the South. In some

Pilgrim children during worship at Plymouth; children from a wealthy southern family dance the minuet.

ways life for African-American children was similar to that of the local European children at the time. Everyone worked hard to survive and had little extra time to read and play. But in other ways, black children had a unique heritage. And in one basic respect, life for most black children would remain different from that of white children for 150 years or so, that is, until the Civil War had been fought and the slaves were set free. What is known about black family life in the colonies will be included in the following pages about growing up in Plymouth and the Chesapeake Bay.

Plymouth – A Small Piece of England

Most of the settlers at Plymouth belonged to the Separatist sect within the Protestant religion known as Puritanism. These Separatists, or Pilgrims, came to America with the idea of starting a new country where they could live the kind of life they believed in. Theirs was a very strict religion, which taught that everyone was born sinful and that children had to be raised in a very rigid way so as to become truly good and worthy of going to Heaven. Their concern for the correct upbringing of their children meant that when the Separatists and other strict religious sects came to America, they usually brought their families with them. About one third of the first settlers in Plymouth were children and young adults. This was unlike settlements in the South, where most of the immigrants were single men in search of adventure and slaves who were usually forced to leave their families behind.

Religion

For the Pilgrims, religion was the most important part of life. As soon as their houses were established, the community built a church. Every part of life was ruled by religion. The day started with family prayers, and prayers were said before, and often after, meals. In the evenings, someone in the family, usually the father, read the Bible aloud while everyone else kept busy. The only songs sung were religious hymns. Children were given names from the Bible, such as Zurishaddai, Mehetable, or Obadiah, or names that expressed ideas that parents were hoping their children would learn, such as Comfort, Temperance, or Forbearance. Sundays were completely devoted to church. There were strict rules about how people could behave. Both adults and children dressed in dark, plain clothes. Children were not allowed to play or sing. This rule was so important that sixteen-year-old Nathaniel Mather, remembering his early childhood, recalled how guilty he felt about breaking it, saying, "Of the manifold [many] sins which then I was guilty of, none so sticks upon me, as that being very young, I was whittling on the sabbath-day; and for fear of being seen, I did it behind the door."

Perfect peace and harmony had to rule. Anyone caught quarreling with a brother or sister on the Sabbath would be severely punished. No work was done, except what was necessary to keep alive. Cows could be milked, for example, and food could be cooked, although the most strictly religious would eat Saturday's cold leftovers on Sunday to keep from doing even that small amount of work.

Going to church on Sunday was the most important event of the week. The youngest children did not attend services, since they could not learn anything from them and would disturb the others. But the older children and adults would

This painting by George Henry Boughton shows Puritans on their way to church. The men are carrying rifles as protection against a surprise attack in the New England forest.

attend a long service in the morning and another one later in the afternoon. White people and black people usually worshiped in the same church, although they sat apart from each other.

Since many people lived too far away to return home between the services, this was an opportunity for friends and relatives to see each other at least once a week, and they would picnic together or invite each other to dinner in between the services (this practice was called "nooning"). Children could see cousins and friends their age, but they were not allowed to play with them. They might talk quietly together if they spoke only of "proper" things.

The parents at Plymouth were quite concerned with the right way to raise their children so that they would grow up to be good Christians. Their religion taught them that when children entered the world they had no notion of right and wrong, and unless they were strictly brought up, they would naturally turn out to be bad people. So the parents watched over their children carefully and were quick to punish them if they caught them doing something they considered wrong. Many, but not all, parents thought that whipping the child with a rod was the best form of punishment. This does not mean that they did not love their children. Their strictness was the only way they knew of to make sure that their children led what they thought was the right kind of life.

Most colonists had come from England, where many holidays were celebrated throughout the year. Aside from Christmas, the English celebrated May Day, with outdoor parties and dancing around a maypole; Easter, with egg hunts and parties; feast days of various saints; and many other special days. But the Pilgrims saw these days as unholy. They recognized that these holidays did not really promote any religious feeling, and people often behaved wildly during them. So their observance was not allowed in the Plymouth Colony. Even children's birthdays passed with no fuss. Weddings were not held in the church and were usually attended only by the couple's close family.

Education

The home and the church were supposed to be where the most important learning took place. One of the main reasons that public schools were first set up in America was so that people could learn enough reading and writing to understand their religion. Children began their studies at around age seven and were at first taught at home, often by their mothers and fathers. A woman with more education or better skill at teaching than the others in her neighborhood would often offer to take in nearby children to teach them how to read, write, and do simple arithmetic. These small learning groups were called "dame schools" and continued for decades in the areas of the country that were too far away from regular schools for children to be able to attend them.

In 1642, the Plymouth Colony passed a law saying that parents were required to teach their children to read. Five years later, a second law said that every town with more than fifty houses had to have a school. Many subjects were taught in those schools, but there was usually some reference to religion. When children learned their alphabet, they memorized a rhyme for each letter. In *The New-England Primer,* published in America around 1690, for example, the letter *A* had the rhyme:

> In Adam's fall,
> We sinn'd all.

In learning subtraction, a child might be asked to figure out how much older one person in the Bible was than another. For history, they would use the Bible to learn which kings ruled ancient countries. Geography lessons rarely taught them about their own country; instead, children knew by heart locations of faraway lands mentioned in the Bible.

It was considered important for the slaves' souls to be saved, too. It was not unusual for black and white children to study together in the Plymouth schools.

A	 In ADAM's Fall We finned all.	N	 NOAH did view The old world & new
B		O	Young OBADIAS, DAVID, JOSIAS All were pious.
	Heaven to find, The Bible Mind.		
C	Chrift crucify'd For finners dy'd.	P	PETER deny'd His Lord and cry'd.
D	The Deluge drown'd The Earth around.	Q	 Queen ESTHER fues And faves the *Jews*.
E	ELIJAH hid By Ravens fed.	R	Young pious RUTH. Left all for Truth.
F	The judgment made FELIX afraid.	S	Young SAM'L dear The Lord did fear.

G	 As runs the Glass, Our Life doth pass.	T	Young TIMOTHY Learnt fin to fly.
H	My Book and Heart Must never part.	U	VASTHI for Pride, Was fet afide.
I	JOB feels the Rod,— Yet bleffes GOD.	W	Whales in the Sea, GOD's Voice obey.
K	Proud Korah's troop Was fwallowed up	X	XERXES did die, And fo muft I.
L	LOT fled to *Zoar*, Saw fiery Shower On *Sodom* pour.	Y	 While youth do chear Death may be near.
M	MOSES was he Who *Israel's* Hoft Led thro' the Sea.	Z	ZACCHEUS he Did climb the Tree Our Lord to fee.

25 *

A page from The New England Primer. *Children learned somber lessons along with the letters of the alphabet.*

The other important job of the schools, aside from religious instruction, was to train young people how to become members of their communities. It was the parents' duty to do this, but if they did not do a good job, the law stepped in and required the children to go to school to learn morality, hard work, and the other virtues considered so important to the early settlers.

The charter setting up the first schools in Massachusetts said that they were necessary because the community's leaders were worried about "the great neglect of many parents and guardians in training up their children in learning and labor which may be profitable to the commonwealth." The law said very clearly what parents' duties were in educating their family. Among other things, they had "to once a week (at the least) catechize [examine] their children and servants in the grounds and principles of Religion." Officials observed how parents were dealing with their children, and if they did not approve, they had the power to require the children to go to school (although the law saying that *all* children had to go to school was not passed for almost two more centuries). Education was taken very seriously, because if a child failed to learn how to be good and industrious, the colony would have lost a valuable citizen.

Since parents were told it was their duty to whip their disobedient children to make them behave better, it is no surprise to learn that teachers often did the same. But apparently some parents were not in favor of such strict discipline, because a few teachers, in advertisements hoping to attract new students, said that they did not beat their pupils. Other punishments were used for different "crimes." Children who talked instead of studying would have a gag put in their mouth, and those who did not learn their lessons quickly enough would have to sit on a stool in front of the whole class wearing a dunce cap or a sign saying FOOL hanging on their chest.

It was hard to learn in these early schools. Paper was very expensive and so it was not used for learning and practice. Instead, other materials had to be found. The bark of the birch tree, for example, peels easily and is almost white, so a student with a lead pencil could use it to practice writing. A child with a few rare pennies to spare could buy a slate— like a miniature blackboard—and use this to write on. A goose's thick feathers, called quills, were made into pens.

In this "dame school," women teach children their lessons, as one little boy who has misbehaved stands on a stool wearing a dunce cap.

A hornbook with the Lord's Prayer copied beneath the alphabet.

The end was trimmed off into a point, and when dipped into ink (usually made by boiling dark tree bark in a little water), it could write a fine, delicate line. Every student advanced enough to write in ink would have to carry a knife to trim the pen as the point got dull.

Books were rare and precious, too. Few students could afford the luxury of a book with printed letters to learn the alphabet. Instead, they used a hornbook. This was a single sheet of paper with the alphabet, the letters, and usually a prayer printed on it. This piece of paper was smoothed over a flat piece of wood and then covered with a slice of a cow's horn, cut so thin that it could be read through. The horn was fastened down over the paper with a thin piece of brass hammered in with tiny nails. Then a hole was bored in the brass strip, and the hornbook was hung on a string around the student's neck, ready for use at any time.

All the students, regardless of their ages, were in one large classroom, with one teacher to watch over all of them. They had to shout their lessons as they learned them, so that the teacher could make sure they were all studying instead of talking to each other or daydreaming. The noise must have been deafening as the smallest children shouted out the alphabet and numbers, the larger ones yelled their sums, and the oldest students read long passages from the Bible at the top of their lungs!

The school day was long. Most students started at eight o'clock in the morning, took a break for lunch at eleven, started the afternoon session at one, and were dismissed at four o'clock. Students who lived close to school walked home for lunch, and the rest brought something to eat carried in a pail. The schoolroom was heated by a wood stove. On winter afternoons, the teacher would remind the students whose turn it was to arrive early at the school the next day and start the stove in the cold, dark schoolroom.

Teachers were paid by the community, which usually had barely enough money for the salary. To save on the teacher's living expenses, the families often took turns having the teacher stay with them for a month or so at a time. Very few communities had enough money to buy supplies for the school. There were no blackboards, globes, books, or sometimes even desks. Students shared long benches with each other, and often used books that their parents had carefully saved from their own school days. "Primers" introduced reading, and "sum-books" taught arithmetic. Penmanship was carefully taught, and children could show their beautiful handwriting with a demonstration page of sentences written with curlicues and fancy designs.

After a child had mastered the basics of education, a decision had to be made: Would this child continue going to school, leave to help at home, or get a job? For almost all girls, the decision was to leave school. It was not considered important for a girl to learn any more than reading, writing, and simple arithmetic. For most boys, the same choice was made. The few who continued studying were the sons of the wealthy, who could afford to hire servants to do the work that the child in school would normally be doing. These scholars studied Latin and Greek, more advanced arithmetic, and other subjects. The few girls who went to school past the first years rarely studied these subjects. They usually went to a "finishing school" to learn French, music, and drawing. They might also study more advanced reading and writing; the first English grammar books published in America were for girls.

Compared to the rest of the Western world at the time, the colonies did not do a bad job of education. In 1660, only a little more than half the men who left wills in New England could write enough to sign their own names to them. (Anyone who did not know how to write his or her own name would have to make a cross or other mark on the line instead of a signature.) By 1710, this number had grown to almost three fourths, and by 1790, nearly all the wills left by men were signed. Naturally, with a smaller number of girls getting educated, their situation was not as good. Fewer than one third of the women who left wills before 1670 could write their names, and in all the rest of the colonial period, this number never even rose to one half of the women.

But education was considered very important for the lucky few chosen to learn more than the basics. As early as 1636, Boston set aside one half of all its money to found Harvard, the first university in the colonies. Boys who had studied Latin and Greek could enter Harvard when they were fourteen years old. Fourteen was the age at which boys were considered old enough to choose a profession and to become more serious about life. A man named Thomas Shepard wrote the following to his fourteen-year-old son, who was starting Harvard in 1672:

> . . . remember . . . that tho' you have spent your time in the vanity of Childhood; sports and mirth, little minding better things, yet that now, when come to this ripeness of Admission to the College, that now God and man expects you should putt away Childish things: now is the time come, wherein you are to be serious, and to learn sobriety [being reasonable], and wisdom in all your ways which concern God and man.

Families

Since most of the settlers in New England had left Europe to start a new kind of life in the "New World," it is not surprising that they were eager to have many children to

V.

The giddy Girl.

Miss Helen was always too giddy to heed
  What her mother had told her to shun;
For frequently over the street, in full speed,
  She would cross where the carriages run.

And out she would go, to a very deep well,
  To look at the water below;
How naughty! to run to a dangerous well,
  Where her mother forbade her to go!

One morning, intending to take but one peep,
  Her foot slipp'd away from the ground;
Unhappy misfortune! the water was deep,
  And giddy Miss Helen was drown'd.

Stories like this one about "The Giddy Girl" taught children harsh lessons about what would happen if they did not do what they were told.

populate their new home. Men and especially women married at a younger age than people in Europe did. They usually had their first baby within one and a half years of the marriage. They continued having babies about once every two years until their late thirties or early forties. You would think that this meant that everyone had a huge family with many brothers and sisters, but many of the babies—about one in four—died before they reached adulthood (this is about the same number as died in England at that time). And young people usually left home earlier than they do today.

Also, many times, parents did not live to see their children grow up. Almost one in four children had lost at least one parent by the time they were five years old. By the age of thirteen, half of the children had lost one or both parents, and almost three fourths had lost one or both by the time they reached adulthood. Very few widows and widowers remained single long; it was simply too hard for one person to run a household and support the family at the same time. Many children grew up in stepfamilies.

Slave families were even more disrupted. Many times, children were sold as soon as they were old enough to leave their mothers, and husbands and wives could be separated as well. Even when families stayed together, the parents did not have final authority over their children. The word of the slaveholder was law.

Disease

Death also separated families more than it does today. Without refrigeration, food often spoiled, and bad food combined with a diet without many vegetables or much milk made people weak. So when disease started spreading, many more people died than would have if they had eaten better and known more about medicine.

The first to die were usually the babies, whose defenses were weak, and people who were already sick from another illness. No one really knew what to do with sick people, so they tried making medicines out of the herbs around them. Some of them worked, but many more did not. Doctors also would "bleed" people, using small wormlike creatures, called leeches, that live in the water and attach themselves by their mouths to anything that wades through their ponds, sucking their blood. Doctors in Europe, and later in the Americas, thought that the loss of a small amount of blood would help almost any illness, so they carried leeches with them to bleed their patients.

For children, there were dangers that are not as common today. Diseases such as diphtheria, smallpox, yellow fever, and scarlet fever would sweep through the colony, sometimes killing whole families at a time. Anyone who survived one of these illnesses would not usually get it again, so older children and adults who had lived through one epidemic were safe. But the next time the sickness came through, many of the very young, who had been born after the last epidemic, would get sick and die.

Because of these problems with nutrition and medicine, people did not live quite as long as they do today, but compared to Europe during the same period, they were healthy. The difficult part was surviving the childhood illnesses. Once they had done this, people could expect to live almost as long as they do today. However, women risked their lives giving birth. And those who survived were often so worn out from having babies that they lived only into their sixties.

The very religious colonists had mixed feelings about illness. On the one hand, it was dreadful to see their babies suffer and die. But many of them also believed that illness was God's way of punishing humanity, and that it was a sin to go against His will and try to cure the sick. Nonetheless, even so deeply religious a man as the famous preacher Cotton Mather believed in "variolation," an early type of vaccination. (He learned about variolation from his slave, Onesimus.) Children were given a small dose of an illness in the hope that they would get only slightly sick from it, and from then on have immunity against the more severe form of the disease.

Aside from illness, there were many causes of injury that few people have to worry about today. To be sure, there were no cars to cause accidents, but there were ladders and stairs and farming dangers and falling trees. And since there was no plumbing, people had to have wells or live near streams that young children could fall into. Fires were kept burning all day and night, and busy parents trying to work and care for several children at once could not be expected to keep as close an eye on the littlest ones as today's parents do. Older brothers and sisters had an important responsibility in looking after the younger children.

Parents and Children

How parents and children felt about each other varied tremendously from one family to another, just as it does today. Although most families in Plymouth consisted of a father, a mother, and two to four children in the house at any one time, some families had several generations all under one roof. Some parents were afraid that they would love their children so much that they would spoil them. While their religion said that children were born sinful and only a strict upbringing could purify them, many parents were tender and loving. A law passed in 1648 says that a "stubborn or rebellious son . . . which will not obey the voice of his Father, or the voice of his Mother" must be put to death, but as far as anyone knows, this law was never enforced. So, to avoid spoiling their children, many parents sent them to live with another family (usually relatives) who could be counted on to train them properly and treat them with kindness, but to punish them if they misbehaved.

No matter what kind of family they lived in, children took an important part in the finances of the household. Aside from the work they did at home, many children earned money to support the family. Children would sometimes be sent out to learn a trade and live with their teacher: This was called "apprenticeship." Often, the parents tried to find a job that the child enjoyed. Usually a child would be at least ten years old before becoming an apprentice, but there were cases of even six-year-olds being forced to start working for another person. Often, the contract signed between the parents and the apprentice's master would state that the child had to be provided with an education, and the law made it clear that the child could not be overworked or treated harshly.

Chesapeake– A Hard Place to Live

If life in the Plymouth Colony seems hard to us today, conditions in the early years of the Chesapeake area were even more difficult. Few of the original settlers in that area had any intention of founding a New World. The white people had come to the Americas because they wanted to get rich quickly in the tobacco fields, and almost all the black people had been brought over against their will. The immigrants were mostly young men. The few women who arrived came as indentured servants. Indentured servants were people who wanted to cross the ocean but did not have enough money to pay their way. So someone else would pay for the ticket, and the indentured servant had to work for them until they had earned enough to pay them back. This usually meant that they were not allowed to get married until they had paid their debt. So by the time they were free to marry, many of them were too old to have children.

Few children were born, and many of them died, since living conditions were extremely unhealthy. In 1625, more than half the married couples had no living children, and most of the families with children had only one or two.

A tobacco plantation in Virginia. From the start, whites depended on blacks to do the hard work of cultivating tobacco: weeding, plowing, tending the plants, and guarding against worms, insects, and frost.

Disease

The Chesapeake area of Virginia and Maryland was, and still is, hot and humid. In this climate, diseases such as cholera, yellow fever, and malaria would frequently sweep through the colony, killing whole families at a time. There were many more orphans than in the Plymouth Colony. And since so many people of all ages would die in the epidemics, many of these orphans had no aunts or uncles to move in with (grandparents were practically unheard of). So they were sent to distant cousins or other relatives who could take care of them. Even distant family relationships became important.

People died so fast, in fact, that the number of deaths was higher than the number of births. For example, about 30,000 Europeans arrived in Maryland between the years 1634 and 1681, but in 1681, whites in that area numbered only 19,000. Between 1635 and 1699, more than 80,000 Europeans emigrated to Virginia from Europe, but in 1700, the white population there was only 60,000. A few of these settlers had returned to Europe, but many of them had died. The numbers of black people who died is unknown, but it was certainly even harder for them to survive than for white people.

Without the slave trade, and without the money that made it possible for the plantation owners to keep buying huge numbers of Africans, the black population would certainly have disappeared. The white population remained nearly stable only because people kept flooding into the colony, lured by the promise of the wealth to be made in the tobacco fields.

Land of Tobacco

The situation was so desperate that the tobacco companies realized that they were in danger of losing their investment in the lands of the Chesapeake, so they started helping out the settlers. They advertised in England for "tobacco brides"—young women who would agree to travel to America and marry a settler there, sight unseen. If they married within a year of their arrival, the tobacco company

A slave keeps flies from the plates of southern plantation owners.

would pay for their trip. After a few years there were more marriages and more children than before.

The company also helped people build better houses than the miserable shacks the first settlers had to be content with. Since it was so hot, one of the first changes the settlers made in their houses as soon as they could afford it was to move the kitchen to a building separate from the main house.

That way the heat of the fire would not make the rest of the house too warm. In the grander homes, the kitchen and the dining room would be joined by a long, covered passageway, down which slaves would hurry with serving plates before the food got cold. The cooking was based on English methods, but local ingredients quickly became popular. A visitor noted: "The Bread in Gentlemen's Houses is generally made of Wheat, but some rather choose the Pone, which is the Bread made of *Indian* Meal [cornmeal]."

Houses were built in the middle of the large tobacco fields, and around each house would be the slave quarters, the servants' shacks, the barns, and all the other farm buildings. So the people in the different houses hardly ever saw each other unless they made a special trip to visit. With houses so far apart, and with so many babies dying, the children who were left must have been very lonely. Up until a certain age (usually the early teens), it was considered proper for black and white children to play together, but as soon as the parents decided that they were too old for this, they were not allowed to socialize at all.

Rich and Poor

Of course, there were both rich and poor people in New England, but the differences were not nearly so great as in the South. By the year 1700, there were a few large, grand homes in the Chesapeake area, with the rest of the population living in small, miserable shacks that could be easily torn apart and moved around the tobacco fields. Not very much is known about the lives of the poorer farmers, since they could rarely read and write, and so left few letters and other records for us to study. Also, their movable houses tended to disintegrate, so it is hard to know exactly how they lived. What is certain, however, is that the lives children led in the mansions and in the tobacco shacks were as different from each other as they could be.

Slaves and Masters

There were many more blacks in the South than in the North. Some of them were free, but most were enslaved. At first, there were few slaves in the area. In 1671, slaves made up only 5 percent of the population of Virginia, but by 1700, this number had grown to 20 percent. In another fifty years, 40 percent—almost half the population—would be enslaved. In South Carolina, there were more blacks (mostly slaves) than whites after 1710.

As soon as they were able to work (at about age six or seven), slave children would start doing chores in the house, running errands, helping in the kitchen, and taking care of white children not much younger than themselves. By age ten or eleven, most slave children were considered old enough to work in the fields, and they joined the adults in the hot labor of working tobacco, cotton, or sugarcane, often for twelve or thirteen hours a day. It was this hard work by black slaves that made life in the big houses possible for white landowners and their families.

The large homes were grand indeed. Not only were there separate rooms for different purposes (bedrooms, living rooms, game rooms, studies) but often the children would have a separate dining room and they would eat with their parents only on special occasions. The grandest homes

A young boy sits alone on the hearth in the bare slave quarters his family calls home.

would have a separate ballroom for use when the family held parties. These usually took place once or twice a year.

The families that could not afford such lavish entertainment still managed to have a good time occasionally. Since much of the work of tobacco farming was easier when people worked together, groups of men would travel from farm to farm to help each other out. Their wives and children would go with them, the women and girls spending all day cooking huge meals for the hungry men and boys. If anyone had energy left at the end of the day, someone would play the fiddle and people could dance.

Churchgoing

The distance between homes, along with the fact that most of the English immigrants were Anglicans (whose religion, while important, was not the center of their lives as it was for the Separatists, Puritans, Quakers, and most other sects of the North), made the social side of churchgoing even more important than its religious purpose. People hardly waited for the service to be over before they started gossiping and catching up on the news. They did not observe the Sabbath as strictly as the Northerners, and would often have parties on Sunday after church. Children could play together and have a chance to get to know each other better. Members of slave families who had been sold to different owners could spend at least a short time together.

The Christian religion was important to the members of the slave community, and not just for social reasons. They were not allowed to practice the religions they had followed in Africa, and many Christians thought it was important to convert as many of these "heathens" to Christianity as possible for the good of their souls. Some slaveholders made sure that the new Christians heard over and over again the parts of the Bible that tell people to be humble and to obey instructions. Starved of the spiritual life that had been so important in their homeland, many of these converts became even more religious than the people who introduced them to Christianity.

Travel

People making a journey had to count on strangers treating them well, since inns were few and far between. If they were not taken in by someone, travelers would be in danger from wild animals or unfriendly people. Since the pilgrims in New England intended to settle for a long time in their new home, many of them made an effort to develop friendly relationships with the Native Americans of their area. But in the South almost from the beginning, Europeans and Native Americans clashed. So at the start of the colonial period, the new settlers tended to travel in groups.

Homeowners would be willing to find a stranger a place to sleep indoors where it was safer than in the woods, knowing that at some time they would probably have to ask some other person for the same favor. Robert Beverley, who traveled in the Virginia area in 1705, said, "The Inhabitants are very courteous to Travellers, who need no other Recommendation but that of being human Creatures. A Stranger has no more to do, but to inquire upon the Road, where any Gentleman, or good Housekeeper lives, and there he may depend upon being received with Hospitality."

Children learned this hospitality early in their lives. In the homes of the poorer people, who usually did not have a separate bedroom, any chance visitor would not only eat but also sleep with the family. On cold nights, the whole family and the guest would often sleep together in the same bed to keep warm!

Home Life
The Anglicans had different ideas about bringing up children than their neighbors to the North. They did not, like the Puritans, think that children were born sinful, needing constant attention and training to become productive

A young woman receives a music lesson on the pianoforte, a common instrument found in wealthy southern homes.

adults. When conditions improved enough for parents to relax and begin enjoying their children, rather than worrying constantly about them dying, their main goal was for their children to be "brought up in Civility good litterature and the feare of God." They were much more easygoing about discipline than Northerners, and visitors from the North and even from England were shocked at what they thought was the parents' spoiling of their children. In contrast to the whipping thought necessary to make a Puritan child behave, one man from Maryland wrote about his stepson, "I tried various experiments upon him (except the Rod [whip] which he never felt in his life or even a slight slap of my hand)."

Many parents seem to have enjoyed their children's company. Eliza Custis, the step-granddaughter of George Washington, recalled a delightful incident from her 1770s childhood, showing a tolerance of childish antics that would surely have shocked the straitlaced Puritans:

> I can now remember standing on the table when not more than three or four years old, singing songs which I did not understand—while my father & other gentlemen were often rolling in their chairs with laughter— & I was animated to exert myself to give him delight. . . . My Mother who could not help laughing, used to retire & leave me to the gentlemen, where my father's caresses made me think well of myself.

Boys and Girls

In the wealthier families, boys and girls were treated quite differently from each other. The women and girls managed the house, the garden, and the small animals, such as chickens. As soon as they could keep up with the men, the boys helped with the outside chores. And when it was time for the children to leave home for marriage, their parents gave them appropriate gifts to help them get started. The boys often received land and the girls housekeeping equipment. In addition, when they could afford it, the parents gave the young couple money, with the bride's parents usually donating about half as much as the groom's.

When they were small, both boys and girls were allowed to roam freely through the wide-open spaces of the coastal South. They played games together, taking advantage of the warm climate to run, climb trees, play marbles, and skip rope. But by the time they reached the age of ten years or so, they were separated, with the boys still playing outside and the girls confined indoors. In fact, it was considered improper, at least among the middle- and upper-class families, for young people even to see members of the opposite sex who were not their close relatives. If a boy brought a male friend home for a visit, the girls were supposed to leave the room unless their mother or aunt was present, and even when they were properly chaperoned and allowed to stay, they could not speak to the boy in a voice too quiet for the adults to hear.

As some people grew more prosperous in the eighteenth century, the girls in these families began to be even more secluded at home, since they had servants and slaves who did most of the outdoor work for them. The only time young people of the upper and middle classes could see each other was during visits to relatives or at dances. Since most of the wealthy landowners lived far apart from their neighbors of the same social class (few of them would consider socializing with people of the lower classes), visits could last a long time. A girl or boy would travel, usually on horseback or by carriage, to the home of a relative or friend and there become part of the family for several weeks, or even months.

Dances were exciting events. All the landowning families for miles around would dress in their best clothes, often specially made for the occasion, and travel to the home of the

Neighbors and friends have gathered for a ball at a wealthy plantation house in the South. The elegant clothing of the guests shows that some colonists brought their aristocratic ways with them to the colonies.

family hosting the event. There the children would play, taking advantage of the unusual opportunity to have a lot of young people together in the same place. Their parents were often too busy to keep a close eye on them, and the children got into wild games and had many adventures. The older children and adults would dance, usually to the music of a fiddle, until suppertime, when everyone would have a chance to sit and talk, catching up on the news. Of course, the older people would keep a sharp eye on the young people, but they usually pretended not to see if a boy and a girl secretly held hands or whispered together. Girls could marry at age sixteen without their parents' consent, and boys at twenty-one (they had to be old enough to support a family). But almost everyone made sure their parents approved of the match before getting engaged. Instead of going home after the dance was over, many times people would stay overnight, and even two or three days.

Education

Unlike the residents of Plymouth, who were determined that everyone learn enough reading and writing to "save their souls," the residents of the southern colonies were much less concerned with education. In fact, the governor of Virginia said in 1670, "I thank God there are in Virginia no free schools nor printing, and I hope we shall not have, for learning hath brought disobedience and heresy into the world." But others wanted to make sure that not only their own children, but all the white residents of the area had at least some schooling. Late in the colonial period, slaveholders and other whites began to be frightened at the thought of slaves' learning to read and perhaps sending each other written plans for an uprising. Many of the southern colonies passed laws making it illegal to teach black people—both slaves and free—to read.

By the end of the colonial period, some of the counties provided free education for all white children, and in cases where they did not, sometimes people would leave money in their wills to establish schools for the children whose parents could not afford it. Occasionally, parents would get together and hire a teacher for all the white children in the area. George Washington was one of the children educated in one of these "old field-schools," as they were called. Some Germans in Maryland provided schooling in German to keep their cultural heritage alive. But even so, many fewer children in the South went to school than did children in the North.

As in New England, most girls did not go beyond simple reading, writing, and arithmetic. But the education was mostly successful. By the eighteenth century, about half the women and two thirds of the men could read and write, at least a little. Of course, some families were not satisfied with the schools available to them, preferring the more traditional schools in Europe. In Maryland, where many Catholics settled, some wealthy Catholic families sent their children to France to complete their education; Protestants often sent their children to England. One little girl named Ursula Byrd was sent to live in a boarding school in 1685, when she was only four years old. These parents believed the extra "polish" of a European education was a definite help in fitting their children into society.

Wealthier families often paid for private tutors. The tutor took over the children's discipline, not just their schooling. It was the tutor, not the parents, who would decide where a child could go, when a boy was old enough to get a gun, or when a girl could learn to ride a horse, and so forth. The tutor would live with the family until the children were grown, sometimes becoming almost part of the family. So it was important to find just the right sort of person for the job. In 1766, Richard Corbin of Virginia wrote to a friend in England asking for help in finding a tutor. He had to be "an honest man well skilled in the languages, that writes a good hand, and is thoroughly acquainted with arithmetick and accounts."

At first, the southern boy who learned enough Latin and Greek to go to college had to go to Europe or New England to complete his education. But in 1693, the South's first college, the College of William and Mary, was founded. As was the case with Harvard, boys could enter William and Mary at age fourteen if they were well prepared enough in their studies.

Girls could also continue their education, but it was not Latin and Greek that they learned. All well-brought-up young ladies were expected to know how to sing, play an instrument, paint, and dance. If their mothers could not or did not want to teach them, they often spent a year or two at a boarding school, either in America or in Europe, learning these skills that were to become so important to them in their adult lives.

For people who could not afford these luxuries, education was a simpler matter. Slaves started working at a very young age, either in the fields or in the house. Free blacks usually learned the same trade as their parents, in almost every case farming. Boys who had to grow up to work with their hands were taught in the practical tradition of apprenticeship, often living with relatives while they learned a trade. Girls were rarely apprenticed, since it was assumed that they would marry and their husbands would support them. But occasionally a girl would stay with a friend or relative who was especially skilled at needlework or spinning to learn how to do these important tasks.

Recreation

Most of the people of the South did not feel, as did many of their neighbors in New England, that play was a dangerous activity, distracting children from the correct pursuit of religion. Instead, certain kinds of recreation were encouraged, at least among the upper classes, since they helped young people form the social contacts that would become important to them later in life. As soon as children could sit on a saddle, they were taught to ride. Upper-class girls had to use the much more difficult sidesaddle method. Boys raced horses, hunted, and played cards with the men.

Children also had games and toys made just for them. Archaeologists digging in Williamsburg, Virginia, have found many toys: miniature soldiers and cannons, store-bought marbles, musical instruments too small for an adult to use, tops, whirligigs, and "bilbo-catchers" (a cup on the end of a stick, with a ball attached to it by a string).

Many of the recreational activities involved groups. Most communities had a fiddler to play at dances and at parties. People were fond of going to plays, and by 1752, Williamsburg had two playhouses.

The more easygoing Southerners did not prohibit celebrations of special days, the way the Northerners did. Weddings were often the occasion for a big party. William Parks's cookbook, written in 1742, has an elaborate recipe for a decorated wedding cake. Religious holidays were not ignored, either. In 1686, a Frenchman named Durand was traveling through the Chesapeake area and joined in with a Christmas party. He said of his host, "Colonel *Fitzhugh* showed us the largest Hospitality. He had Store of good Wine and other Things to drink, and a Frolic ensued. He called in three Fiddlers, a Clown, a tight rope Dancer and an acrobatic Tumbler, and gave us all the Divertisement [fun] one would wish."

On special occasions, slaves were allowed to have parties as well. This was not because the slaveholders wanted them to have a good time, but it was a way to make them at least a little more content with their lives. They would be issued some meat (a pig or young steer) and some drink, and would be allowed to take a day or two off. When a number of slaves from the same region of Africa were present, traditional songs might be sung. However, the slaveholders were generally careful to keep people apart who had been taken from the same region in Africa. They were afraid that the slaves might talk together in a language their owners could not understand, and perhaps plan together to run away or revolt. So the slaves lost many of their traditional languages, songs, and customs.

———

The children who grew up in the American colonies had many different life experiences. A slave child in Maryland and a Puritan child in Massachusetts would have little in common. Children in cities, children in the country; children in the North, children in the South; Puritans and Anglicans; black and white; boy and girl—many of the differences between groups in modern America can be traced back to our colonial beginnings.

Fradin, Dennis B. *The Thirteen Colonies.* Chicago: Childrens Press, 1988.

Kallen, Stuart. *Life in the Thirteen Colonies 1650–1750.* Minneapolis: Abdo & Daughters, 1990.

McGovern, Ann. . . . *If You Lived in Colonial Times.* New York: Scholastic, 1992.

Perl, Lila. *Slumps, Grunts, & Snickerdoodles: What Colonial America Ate & Why.* Boston: Houghton Mifflin, 1979.

Smith, Carter, ed. *Daily Life: A Sourcebook on Colonial America.* Brookfield, Conn.: The Millbrook Press, 1991.

———. *The Explorers and Settlers: A Sourcebook on Colonial America.* Brookfield, Conn.: The Millbrook Press, 1991.

Warner, John F. *Colonial American Home Life.* New York: Franklin Watts, 1993.

Bibliography

Albin, Mel, and Dominick Cavallo, eds. *Family Life in America, 1620–2000.* New York: Revisionary Press, 1981.

Bremner, Robert H., ed. *Children and Youth in America: A Documentary History.* Vol. I: 1600–1865. Cambridge, Mass.: Harvard University Press, 1970.

Calvert, Karin. *Children in the House: The Material Culture of Early Childhood, 1600–1900.* Boston: Northeastern University Press, 1992.

Demos, John. *Past, Present, and Personal: The Family and the Life Course in American History.* New York: Oxford University Press, 1986.

Earle, Alice Morse. *Child Life in Colonial Days.* New York: Macmillan, 1932.

———. *Home Life in Colonial Days.* New York: Macmillan, 1898.

Fleming, Sandford. *Children and Puritanism: The Place of Children in the Life and Thought of the New England Churches, 1620–1847.* New Haven, Conn.: Yale University Press, 1933.

Greenleaf, Barbara Kaye. *Children Through the Ages: A History of Childhood.* New York: McGraw-Hill, 1978.

Hart, Albert Bushnell. *Colonial Children.* New York: Macmillan, 1925.

Hawes, Joseph M., and N. Ray Hiner, eds. *American Childhood: A Research Guide and Historical Handbook.* Westport, Conn.: Greenwood Press, 1985.

Hawke, David Freeman. *Everyday Life in Early America.* New York: Harper & Row, 1988.

Johnson, Clifton, *Old-Time Schools and School-Books.* Macmillan, 1904. Reprinted by Gale Research Company: Detroit, 1982.

Morgan, Edmund S. *The Puritan Family: Religion and Domestic Relations in Seventeenth-Century New England.* New York: Harper & Row, 1944. Revised edition, 1966.

————. *Virginians at Home: Family Life in the Eighteenth Century.* Williamsburg, Va.: Colonial Williamsburg Press, 1952.

Smith, Daniel Blake. *Inside the Great House: Planter Family Life in Eighteenth-Century Chesapeake Society.* Ithaca, N.Y.: Cornell University Press, 1980.

Smith, Wilson. *Theories of Education in Early America, 1655–1819.* Indianapolis: Bobbs-Merrill, 1973.

Sommerville, C. John. *The Rise and Fall of Childhood.* Beverly Hills, Calif.: Sage Publications, 1982.

Stone, Gertrude L., and M. Grace Fickett. *Every Day Life in the Colonies.* Boston: D.C. Heath, 1908.

Williams, Alicia Crane. "Women and Children First." *American Heritage,* vol. XXVIII, no. 5, November/December 1993, pp. 44–47, 73.

Wright, Louis B. *The Cultural Life of the American Colonies, 1607–1763.* New York: Harper Brothers, 1957.

Wright, Louis B., ed. *Newes from the New-World.* Los Angeles: Anderson Ritchies: The Ward Ritchie Press, 1946.

Index